THE VAST EMPTY

TURIYA

Copyright © 2022 by Turiya

All rights reserved.

This book or any portion thereof may not be reproduced or used in any manner whatsoever without the express written permission of the respective writer of the respective poem except for the use of brief quotations in a book review.

The writer of the respective work holds sole responsibility for the originality of the poem and The Write Order is not responsible in any way whatsoever.

Printed in India

ISBN: 978-93-5565-225-6

First Printing, 2022

The Write Order

Koramangala, Bangalore

Karnataka-560029

THE WRITE ORDER PUBLICATIONS.

www.thewriteorder.com

Dedicated to the Divinity within us - may we all feel It and be guided by It.

Sincere gratitude to my guru Santosh Ma for showing me the way.

To my family and friends who continue to inspire and support me in so many other ways.

TABLE OF CONTENTS

Obsession	- 1 -
Words	- 2 -
Wanderer	- 3 -
The place	- 5 -
Jigsaw	- 6 -
I'm Here	- 7 -
Breath	-8 -
Age	- 9 -
Hours	- 10 -
Oasis	- 12 -
On living	- 14 -
Death	- 15 -
Knowing	- 16 -
Seeking	- 17 -
Anticipation	- 18 -
Fallen	- 19 -
Stars	- 20 -
The Strand	- 21 -
Air	- 22 -
Serendipity	- 23 -
Smoke up	- 24 -
Fragrance	- 25 -
Hiding	- 26 -
Dreams	- 27 -
Ending	- 28 -
Gone	- 29 -
Wander Deep	- 31 -

Desire	- 32 -
Happiness	- 34 -
Rise	- 36 -
Floating	- 38 -
I Am Whole	- 39 -
Becoming	- 40 -
The Sound	- 42 -
This Moment	- 44 -
Thoughts	- 45 -
Travel Far	- 46 -
Renunciate	- 47 -
Capture	- 48 -
Tears	- 49 -
Final offering	- 50 -
Fragments	- 51 -
The House of Reality	- 53 -
Release	- 54 -
Rescue	- 55 -
Quest	- 56 -
Thoughts	- 57 -
Origami	- 58 -
Perfume	- 61 -
Driftwood	- 63 -
Dive	- 65 -
The Date	- 67 -
The Willows	- 68 -
Saudade	- 71 -
Days Without End	- 72 -
Rain	- 73 -
Memory	- 75 -

Slowing Down	- 77 -
Full Circle	- 79 -
Space	- 85 -
Question	- 86 -
Still	- 88 -
Moon	- 89 -
The Key	- 90 -
Thoughts	- 91 -

Obsession

How comfortably ensconced
you are in my mind,
my love!
As constant as my breath
and the beating of my heart,
You are embedded
in every waking thought
all of which weave themselves
Into a gossamer sheath
that I gently draw over me
every night
Willing myself to dream of you.

You and I,
we travel
Deep in my dreams
into a life we could have had
with each other.
But when I wake up,
I wonder,
would you still fill my mind,
the same way
If you were here by my side?

Words

The words, they stood silently
at the edge of the precipice.
Beautiful words,
profound and independent.
Some were overpowering
with their potency,
others simple and elegant.
And some, just humble and tiny,
they jostled and arranged
into formation.

And when the wind blew right,
or the moon lit up the night,
or when rain fell to earth
on a night heavy
with the fragrance of jasmine,
the words launched themselves
as lyrical poetry
and flew into a waiting heart.

That heart,
was it yours?

Wanderer

If you could be anywhere,
where would you go?
Would you stay there?
How do you know?

Nomads wander
in search of food,
shelter or water.
But you, what is it you are after?

The thing that you seek,
do you know what it is?
Or are you just enthralled
by the idea of perpetual drift?

Is it a person, place or feeling?
Tell me,
my wanderer,
what are you chasing?

There is no anchor to weigh you down,
nor a cage to contain you within.

You were forever free
and on your own,
yet you are running
always
without getting
to any place.

Maybe, the person you seek
lies deep within.
Maybe, the place you want to go
is not on a map,
but in your mind.

And when the adventures end,
and there is no thrill,
all you may want is
for your mind to be still.

Because whatever you are seeking,
if you don't find it where you are,
What you want will always be
just that tiny bit too far!

The Place

Have you discovered the beauty of the place you call 'the mind'?
A place you can be the person you were meant to be,
not the one forced on you.
Where actions have no consequences and beauty is timeless,
where time is still,
Age is irrelevant and rules don't exist.
A place where you can love who you want
and leave when you want to.
Where you can be surrounded by friends or make friends with solitude.
Where you can be free of anchors and bereft of responsibilities.
Where you ride at will with your love, with no destination in sight
and no end in mind.
Where afternoons are spent dreamy and stoned on balmy beaches,
Evenings indulged in wine, romance and music chaperoned by stars,
And the night spent in the arms of your love,
traversing the Milky Way
on each other's bodies.
Where desire is fulfilled,
Passion is spent
and fantasies come alive.
Endlessly and forever
Day after day.
If this is what heaven is,
Take me there right now!

Jigsaw

Is that how it works?
That when you're born,
Your life's journey is ordained
As a magnificent collage
Of experiences and places
Of things that will be done
And dreams that will be conjured.
A tapestry of intersections,
Of paths that will be tread,
Of people that will be met,
Of a life that will unfold
With a million connections forged.
This glorious collage,
Dismantled and scattered
Like a sublime jigsaw
Across time and space
For you to go through life,
Gathering the pieces
Into a complex matrix
With a billion dimensions
Interconnected with the collage
Of everyone you met.
So when you find the last piece
And with trembling hands
Complete the puzzle,
I hope that the picture
That emerges is more glorious
And that you lived better
Than you were destined to.

I'm Here

I looked across the room
Through the clutter
Of people
Barely escaping glances,
Almost colliding with conversation.

And I saw you -
Looking
right back
at me!

I asked,
Without words,
Where are you?
You replied,
With a smile,
I'm here.

I asked -
Here? In this place?
In this moment?
In your smile, or in my gaze?

Don't you know, you reply,
I'm in your gaze right now,
Soon I'll be the smile on your lips,
And then, in the flush of your skin,
In the racing of your heart
And in every waking thought.

Breath

They say life is not measured by the number of breaths you take
But in those that take your breath away.
It is not in the moment that you long for
But in the longing, in each moment.
It's not in the hues of the rainbow
But in the blush, as it rises through a face.
It's not in the expressions you show
But in those, you struggle to contain.
Life is not lived in the days that pass
But in those moments, you wish time had forever stopped.
Life was not meant to be lived sleepless amidst city lights
But lying on the grass under the canopy of stars.
Life is in the knowing gaze of a lover
And in the caress that sets your heart on fire.
It's walking in the drizzle of the summer rain
And lying by the warmth of a winter fire.
It's in the smell of woodsmoke carried by the breeze
And in the snowflake landing on the windowsill.
Slow down, my love
And take the time to see
If you are truly living
The life that you should be.

Age

Youth is wasted on the young they say.
Who are 'they', I wonder,
As I stand firm in my forties
And look back on who I wanted to be in my twenties,
Why do I only see
Opportunities not seized,
The unmade choices and the missed chances,
Mistakes that were committed
or the wrong turns taken?
Yet, who is to say
This was not exactly how it was meant to be?
Would 'they' guarantee an outcome
Where I don't ask the same question
At precisely the same age,
but from a different place?

Hours

The hours seem endless
The day stretches on
I think of the places I've been to
And dream of new dawns
The thrill of new sights
scents of a different life
The pleasure of wine
the busyness of being alive
A child rushes in
Forcing me
out of my
reverie
There is milk to be heated
A lunch to be served
Chores to complete
A household to run
Still, I take a moment
And look out
To the sunlit garden
The little flower patch
And the freshly cut grass
Somewhere a couple is laughing
As a present is unwrapped
A dove flies into the sky
A dog chases a cat
The aroma of coffee
Wafts in from next door
Music is played
From across the road

Suddenly, my heart feels full
There is light in my soul
Everything I need
I feel around me
Yet, I went looking everywhere
For things
Always within me

Oasis

That oasis you hunt for,
Do you know where it exists?
How far will you travel?
How much will you endure
In your escape to reality?

Do you know where it is,
That place you seek?
Where the sound of your breath
Drowns everything else-
The noise, the clutter
The fatigue of life, fear of death.

Or when you go on a hunt
For that elusive strand
of love and passion
Of purpose and meaning
Embedded in the tangled heap
Of intellect and feeling.

Perhaps what you look for,
You think can be found
Locking eyes with a stranger
In the middle of a crowd?
Or in the freedom of travel
On a well-trodden road
When your destination is known
But you still take a detour?

My love, how long will you try
To capture your shadow
And wander through your head
wrestling your mind
To an ephemeral floor?

When will you realise
You're not your thoughts
Nor are you your actions
Your existence and purpose
Are just an illusion
part of a sublime imagination.

Truth is, you are deep asleep
Just an actor in another's dream
There will come a time
When you will be roused
Be touched by grace
And open your eyes
To be finally dissolved.

On Living

"How long do you want to live?"
My soul asked me,
As I sat by the fire
Searching for meaning
In a glass of wine.
Do I want to live
Well past my prime
Hanging on to memories
And to glorious old times?
Do I want to live
Even as my purpose is done
Or my reason for existence
Comes undone?
Do I want to die
When I am worn and fatigued
Battle faced and
Scarred with age?
Or do I want to go
At the peak of life
Passion in my veins
A heart full of calm
Prayer on my lips
A song in my soul
Surrounded by love?
Perhaps we have it all wrong-
Maybe life is a pause
And death is the journey
And we remain alive
Even when we die.

Death

I wake up from my dream,
Incomplete.
I left behind parts of me in my dream-
like markers in the vast labyrinth,
stretching beyond,
into the ancient,
and into another realm,
Knowing that sleep will bring me back
To this exact same point
To restart,
to chart my next life.

So, is this how we die?

Do we willfully disintegrate,
slowly and subtly,
leaving behind parts of ourselves,
across space and time,
when the mind dissolves in sleep,
And when we travel in our dreams?

Knowing

Of lifetimes crisscrossing
Of historical intersections
Of memories surfacing
Of emotions gnawing
Of knowledge almost revealing
Of search never-ending
In the center of it
My old soul
Tied to the yoke
Of karmic weight
Bears the burden
And drags itself
From one lifetime
To the next.

Seeking

I wake up from my dream,
Seeking.
In my dream, I turn the corner of a familiar path-
But the familiar is gone
and in its place is the unfamiliar
But not unknown.

Five thousand years separate the corner I turned
and the place before my eyes.
The vast ancient that stretches before me
is awash with a golden hue
It is still and quiet,
Like the place in my mind that I struggle to reach,
A place I never want to leave.

I see no one, but I know I am not alone.
A watchful presence surrounds me,
Someone I know,
from the deepest recess of my mind,
but can't remember.

The one who I have searched for
Through the vastness
Through unfamiliar places,
hidden deep within.
Never knowing
but always longing,
always searching.

Anticipation

A single dew drop
Hung on to the rock,
And I sat watching it for hours
Waiting for it to free itself and drop-
Much like the words
Stuck in your heart.
But those words,
What do they want?

Fallen

I walk bare feet
On the soft carpet
Of fallen leaves.
How beautiful it is
To watch them
Sway gently
In the breeze
And fall
One by one
So exquisitely!
Is my life
As sublime
As the falling leaf
Full of grace
Even as it dies?

Stars

I lie down to sleep
Hoping that I will soon rise
To wander amongst the stars
Scattered across the vast skies.

These stars,
they hold my memories
From eons before,
from the time I wasn't born
And beyond,
into the time after I die.

These memories,
they stretch into infinity-
There is no end in sight,
How long will my journey last?
How long before I can finally
Sleep in the stars?

The Strand

The leaf was held by a strand
A single thread of a spider's web
All but invisible
As it swayed with the breeze
Grasping the leaf.

My Beloved,
Is my hope like this silken thread
That anchors me to you?
One that you send
Unfailingly,
Every time,
To my rescue?

Air

The blood that runs in my veins,
It's all mine,
forever contained in me
Till I die.
The air I breathe, it's mine too
But only for a moment.
I give it up to stay alive
And one day it will leave with my life.

And yet
In that moment
And in that breath,
I send out my essence
And breathe in someone else's-
A breath that contains a sigh of relief,
A prayer,
Or the sharp intake of wonder,
Perhaps one of longing,
Maybe of desire?

So my love,
when I am in your presence
And I breathe deep
Am I making you
And that moment
Forever a part
of my life?

Serendipity

You lose your way
And it takes you
Where you were meant to be
A vast echo chamber
Hidden in plain view
Tucked away from reality
Abandoned, empty and quiet.

Your footsteps resounding
Flutter of doves above
A feather floats to you - a quill,
A gift from a djinn.

A doorway opens
A stranger walks in
A connection is forged
Without a single word.

You are precisely
Where you needed to be
For a person,
For a place
For a purpose
For a play of
Destiny.

Smoke Up

Live in this moment
Breathe in its essence
Close your eyes
Let it swirl around in your mind
Like an expanding cosmos
Whirling with heavens
Immersing you with it.
Let it bend your thoughts
And numb your reason
Allow it to leap over the ordinary
And land you in the surreal
Invite the haze to descend
And clear your vision
To see the things lying unseen
Through smokescreens laden with meaning.
Feel the sensation of paper against your skin
Hear the lyrics of the orchestra
And the screams hidden in silence
Notice gestures
That speak louder than words
As you gaze into the heart
sitting across.
Inhale deeply, take it all in
Let your mind unfurl
And welcome the drum roll within.

Fragrance

I travelled through the crowded city
Taking in the chaos,
the clutter
and the din.
The messiness of it all-
People's thoughts,
actions, and feelings,
Evading and colliding.

I walk in the midst of this
Ordered randomness
Overwhelmed and exhausted.

I pass by a temple
Thronging with people
Dense with worry, faith, hope and supplication
Reaching God is also a struggle,
and I'm too tired to battle.

So I turn away,
And as I do
A slender waft floats towards me-
Camphor, incense, rose and jasmine.

So ephemeral and subtle
Like a reminder, a blessing
I close my eyes and memorise this fragrance
My Beloved is never far from me.

Hiding

I hide in the words
written to conceal feelings.
Will you find me at the turn of a phrase,
at the beginning of a full stop, or resting on a hyphen?
Perhaps in the rhythm of lyrics,
or maybe in an italic,
or even hanging from a comma?
Your eyes dart from word to word
As you search for me,
And wonder just where and how
I might reveal myself.

But my love, your eyes just skimmed
Past the space I was waiting in-
I was in the gap between the letters,
and in the silence and the pause.
I was always hiding in plain sight
I am the one
Who can't be contained by words .

Dreams

I float into awareness
I don't know
If I have woken up in my dream
Or if I am dreaming in my sleep
Eons stretch
Between my sleep and my dream
And I am at once
A native of both
But a resident of neither.

Ending

When all was said
And the dust settled
We looked around,
And amongst the debris
Of wounds raw,
Of feelings forgone
And of things
Still left to be said,
We find small treasures
Worthy of nurture.
These we shall keep,
And even the rest
We won't throw.
For who is to know
In the future
There might be
A place, and time
For them to grow.

GONE

I woke up one day
To realise
That the words
Had gone away.

The calm ones
That had captured
And reigned in
Anger and hate,
And slowly but steadily
Tamed,
And dissolved
Them all
Had also left.

The softly whispered words
That gently gathered
Passion and love,
Forgiveness,
Acceptance,
And carried them on delicate wings
To set them free
To wander amongst stars,
Moonlight and galaxies
In the form of song,
Maybe poetry.

All of a sudden,
I feel bereft.

My companion - the words
Have all but abandoned me.
I looked within only to see
That they never really
Belonged to me.

Maybe this is the freedom
I always sought
Through the silence
I become the emptiness
The emptiness
That finally
completes me.

Wander Deep

You travel on your breath
Languidly, steadily
With unseeing eyes focused within-
To reach that place,
Towards the edge of your mind
Near the far reaches of the universe
Into the core of your soul.

Each time you breathe
You get closer to the deep,
The closer you get
The further you reach
Till you bridge the chasm
Between your many lives
And across time and space
When you travel everywhere
By being still
And in one place.

Desire

I felt a deepening sorrow
the day I witnessed
The death of my desire.
What do I live for?
What should I aspire to be?
A weight had been lifted
But the lightness weighed me down!

The tingle of excitement
That cruised through my veins-
Would I ever
feel that again?
Or the anticipation
of desire
about to be fulfilled,
Or the despair of things
that came undone?

Desire was dead
I was about to be free.
The sky of detachment
Beckoned to me.
Elated,
I stepped out of myself
Ready to take
to the open skies

But when I turned around to see
I saw my heart

weeping for me-
For within the ashes of desire
Lay burnt
feelings, emotions
hope and passion.

Interred was so much
That had made me human
Yet, I still was lightyears away
From becoming Divine.

Happiness

I was overcome
With a bliss so sheer
The day I witnessed
The death of my desire.
So much to live for
Without the burden
Or need for aspiration.
A weight had been lifted
The lightness set me free!

A gentle calm
Cruised through my veins
Tempering anger,
Mellowing passion
Soothing the storm that used to be.
Free finally
From anticipation,
from despair
From outcome
And fear of coming undone.

Desire was dead
I was closer to the edge
The sky of detachment
Spread out ahead
Elated,
I stepped out of myself
Ready to take flight.

But when I turned around to see
Emerging from the ashes of desire
I saw divinity
reach out for me.

For interred alongside
Were those feelings, emotions
Hopes and passion.
Those things that had made me human
And had held me
from becoming Divine.

R ISE

I have risen
From a slumber so deep
Into a light
That engulfs me.
Ten thousand bells
Ring in the distance
Clearing my sight
Freeing my mind.

I see glimpses of you
Sublime and deep
A force so powerful
A reflection of me.
We have been travelling now
For five thousand years
Through many lives
Across space,
Beyond time
Creating our destiny
Into eternity.

Memories surface
In every blink of my eyes
A million dreams
Woven intricately
People and places
Battle scenes and scars.
Emotions I reach out to-
I touch and grasp.

And when I look deeply
With unseeing eyes
I feel the flame of wisdom-
A wisp from the past
Reaching out for me.

My Beloved,
We are bound forever-
I am your shepherd
Till the end of our time.
Come with me,
Take my hand
Let me deliver us
From this endless journey
Back into
The Vast Empty!

Floating

I float languidly
Down a river of dreams
On a bed of thoughts
Woven into fantasies
I am like mercury
Formless and silvery
Breaking and merging with ease
At times I am a thought
Sometimes the dream
I weave in and out
Trespassing
Everywhere at once
But nowhere really.

I Am Whole

I look into my soul
And discover the cosmos
I glance at the leaf
And I become it's green
I wander out of the door
And stumble into the universe
I lie down amongst the stars
And I become it's light
I am contained
And yet I am free
I am everything
Still, no trace of me
I am in this moment
Yet I existed forever
I close my eyes
And now I can see
I become aware
Finally, I am one
With Reality.

Becoming

I was my body
I was my vanity
I was my beauty
I was my illusion

Then I became myself
I became my silence
I became my mind
I became my thought
I became my breath

And I escaped

I became the glisten of the dewdrop,
the reflection on the water,
I became the transparency of the dragonfly's wings,
and the rustle of the wind

I became the softness of a breath,
and the radiance of love
I became the kindness of the alms giver,
and the blessing of the beggar

I became the roughness of the stone,
and power of water flowing around
I became the smoothness of the pebble,
it's cool touch against skin
I became the dream of a sleeper,
and the vibrations of a string

I became day
I became night
I became everything
I became nothing
And now I am the light
I am also the Void.

The Sound

Hidden deep within-
Behind the voices of
The birds,
The flow of rivers,
And the noise of life-
Is a Sound

A sound so deep
From the core of yourself
Maybe from deep within the earth
And yet so distant
Like the sound of space,
Rushing into your mind,
A sound so constant
So visceral

Be still
Listen

For it is the sound of light
From a million stars
From galaxies waiting to be discovered

It is the sound of your memory
from all your lives engulfing you

It is the sound of every thought that occurred
The sound of eternal knowledge being revealed

It is the sound of the beginning and
The sound that will remain after the End

It is the sound of creation,
And the sound of existence

It is a whisper of the universe
Murmuring its secret to you

It is the sound of your effort
As you travel into your soul

It is the sound of wisdom
The sound of knowing Yourself

It is the sound of the One Truth
It is the sound of You

This Moment

I live in the moment
Neither burdened by hope
Nor anchored in memory
Nor weighed down by judgement.

Just an observer
Of my unfolding destiny

Let every blink
Be a tiny death

Every day I'll die
A million times
And be reborn
Each time
I open my eyes.

Thoughts

I walk through the garden
Treading on leaves freed by the breeze
My thoughts clamour for attention
And I tiptoe around them
I am walking through the garden,
But perhaps
I am just strolling through my mind.

Sitting now beneath the weeping willow
I watch them fall
A million leaves,
One by one

In the distance I see
Tall, sturdy,
Sparse
Bereft
A tree
Piercing through foliage
Not a leaf on its branches
Beyond life
Beyond death
Beyond thought

In its emptiness lies its beauty
Will that ever be me?

Travel Far

The eyes- they need to travel far
They need to sweep
Over mountains,
Delve into the farthest depths
Of the ocean,
They must sink into the earth's soul
And rise to become air and roam the skies.
Let them go past all horizons-
The ones we know
And even those we imagine
For only when you look beyond and see
Do you fathom
what's within
truly.

Renunciate

I walk on the road that
Leads to the end-
Leaving behind myriad loves,
A life, my family and friends.

The silence cuts through
Drowning the sound of a falling leaf
And the flutter
of a butterfly's wing.

I walk the path all alone-
My heartbeat, it slows down
To keep pace
with my heavy step.

There is no end I realise
And never was there
A beginning either
The road disappears
But the journey continues.

I die a thousand deaths
And each time I am renewed.

Capture

Is it possible to capture beauty with your eyes
or your feelings with just words?
Can you capture the power of a river with your hands
or the magnificence of a mountain with a climb to its summit?
Can you capture eternity in a moment
or time in just the movement of a clock?
Can you capture life with your heartbeat
or passion with your heartache?
Can you capture all of your memories in a fragrance
or your childhood in a single place?
Can you capture adventure through travel,
or freedom through just being set free?
Can you capture peace through meditation
or through a saint the essence of purity?
Can you capture your mind through your thoughts
or your soul with your body?
Why do we try to capture devotion through a ritual,
or divinity in a temple?
Why do we try to capture God in an idol
When there is divinity in your soul?

Tears

I weep, without tears, for my heart
Which breaks itself, into a thousand shards
Without help from anyone,
and without cause or reason.

I pick up each sliver,
so delicate and fragile, almost porcelain-like
And lay it gently on my palm.
I stare intently at each piece
Willing it to give up its secrets
And to reveal the reason for its distress.

But with each shard I pick up
I only see myself reflected
And the wounds I inflicted.
Suddenly, invisible tears start to well
And roll down my face,
For I know
I am both
The reason and the cause
For my broken heart.

Final Offering

My Beloved,
First, I emptied my mind
At your shrine
Then I wrenched out my heart
And made you an offering
My scorched soul
I burnt it to cinders
And gave you the ashes
Now all that is left
Is just an empty shell
Containing my breath
Here, I offer you that as well
So that
Every last trace of me
Can finally
And completely
Cease to be.

Fragments

I exist in ten thousand beings-
In the people around,
The trees, dust and stones,
In still waters,
And the river
As it flows,
And yet none of them is me.

I exist in ten thousand feelings-
In the blessing of one who asks,
In the gratitude of one who receives,
In the safety of a hug,
The acceptance of a smile,
And in the invitation
In someone's eyes.

Sometimes I am a word spoken out of turn,
At times, a memory waiting to be formed.
I am in that accidental graze of the hand,
In the impulse that was acted upon,
And yet, none of them is me.

I hold a mirror to my soul
It cracks and shatters-
A thousand pieces lie scattered on the floor.
Each one reflects
A tiny piece of life
Yet none of them
Is mine.

I keep searching for myself,
Not knowing where to look
Hoping to be contained
And still be free
I know I am blessed
And yet
Sorrow envelopes me.

The House of Reality

In the house of living
Through the arched doorways of expectation
Wandering into rooms lit by the warm glow of happiness
Through the passageways of despair
And down the steps of memories
I make way into the garden of dreams
Sit on the cold stone bench of reality
And slowly sip the drink of reflection
Around me, the mist of lost chances rolls in
And settles as dense fog of missed opportunities
And there, I blew out the last candle of hope.

Release

Night after night,
across the world,
people like you and I
lie awake;
Trying to drown ourselves in sleep
Yet staying afloat
On pillows of broken dreams;
Lost in mists of fading youth
Our hopes receding like the ebb of tides
Fearful of what the morning might bring.

Like caged birds
our souls & minds long for release
Will we die,
full of despair,
Or free ourselves
And fly into the open air?

Rescue

My Beloved,
come and rescue me
From the wreckage
Of my own creation
Of crushed feeling
And mangled emotions
Help me clean it out
So nothing remains
And I restart my journey
With each breath
To your name.

Quest

The tears,
they just don't stop
Why am I weeping
What have I lost
What am I seeking
Will I be found
Always travelling
Never reaching
Each time I die
I am reborn
This journey is endless
Yet I carry on.

Thoughts

Some thoughts don't need the liberation of words
They exist alone
by themselves
Like distant stars
In far off galaxies
Majestic in their solitude
Lofty in their isolation
Holding a primordial truth
Defying description
Escaping the trap of the haughty word
which try to reign them in
A million intellects turn their gaze towards them
Yet these thoughts
Lie deep, still
And silent
Never giving up their secrets
Loyal till the end
True to their source

So my love,
remember this when you ask,
tell me what you're thinking.

ORIGAMI

I don't play poker.
But I like the term "fold."
There is a finality to it that closes all doors,
nothing further will happen,
at least not for you,
and not for now.
That you have accepted the hand that fate has dealt
and with stoicism hopefully you will move on.
You can come back and try again.
But for now, this is it.

And then there is "fold" in origami.
This fold indicates creation, and movement, and change.
Every fold is a new possibility.
It will lead to something
Whether you fold absentmindedly
Or with intent
And towards a purpose.
Whatever you do,
you will still create something
That people can recognize or define,
or something that escapes definition.
You can stop
when you think you have folded enough,
and it will remain in that state,
pregnant with potential,
maybe waiting for you to come back to it later.
You may abandon it altogether
and it will still remain - a creation.

Much like friendships and relationships
that adorn our life's journey.
Some have been folded with intent,
purposefully,
towards a shape and definition.
Some halted midway
Because any more folding would have destroyed
Its structure, beauty and meaning.
Some aborted hastily
because you knew the alarming shape it was taking.

And then there are some
Which you keep folding
Intricately, and
Delicately, and
Slowly,
Always slowly,
Over time,
Over years,
Across continents.
Every fold adding a new dimension - subtle and sublime,
adding meaning and joy.
It will always be a work in progress,
defying all logic, definition and rules.
Limitless.
And it will remain eternally cherished
and beautiful,
its beauty enhanced
with
every
fold.

That is the one,
above all,
that defines your being.
It has no equivalent in poker
And you can never fold this.

Perfume

A strain of music wafting from an open window on an early autumn evening,
the mystic blue of the sky at dusk as it converges slowly into the inky black of night,
the muted yellow glow from an upstairs window filled with hints of intimacy
Evidence of everyday life.
Yet they evoke a feeling of longing within you -
A longing for what?
For whom?

You cannot define let alone understand it.
Perhaps it triggers a memory-
A memory of languid summer afternoons
Spent in the arms of a beloved,
or that moment when a stray word
Or a glance
Or a poem (was it stray?)
Set a relationship down a new path.

Maybe time has changed everything.
Maybe there are no afternoons,
perhaps no beloved,
perhaps no love,
or maybe that new path the relationship took,
led to despair and desolation.
Or maybe everything is still the same -
The beloved is just older,

the early thrill of relationship now long burdened with domesticity
And settled into a steady, deadening rhythm -
Everything tinted sepia with age, experience
And the crushing realization
Of lost youth and of unfulfilled dreams.

Those days and those moments were thrilling-
Like a newly opened bottle of perfume - heady and addictive.
The allure of the fragrance captivating just like that moment,
and the complexity of the notes, much like those feelings.
You breathed deeply the fragrance
and committed it to your memory.

And yet, like all things committed,
it gets lost in the vast and intricate filing system of the mind-
like the precious treasures of the museum store -
Too valuable to be discarded
But too much to be displayed,
Always there, rarely referenced.

And now, as you pass by that window,
and when you notice the sky
Or hear that particular strain of music,
the memory explodes from its cocoon
And startles you with its vivacity and freshness.
Sharp and overwhelming,
Like the fragrance that floods the room
When the perfume bottle is dropped
And shatters itself
Into a million pieces.

Driftwood

Like driftwood
I ride the ocean waves
Placid, lulled by the warm sun
Water embracing me
A womb created
By joining sky and sea.
In it, I float languidly.

Day turns to night
The sun bids goodbye
Above me a billion stars explode
Somewhere a soft breeze blows
I continue my aimless ride
No thoughts in my mind
The calm reflected in my soul.

Tomorrow, the weather may turn
A storm may rage
And I could break.
My life could end
As suddenly as it began
But then,
I can't remember being born
And I won't know if I am dead and gone
My earliest memories were
When I was three,
Perhaps that's when life
began for me.

Yet, here I am now
Gentle water beneath me
A starlit night above
All the treasures I need
Are in my head and heart
My soul holding me afloat.

Maybe this is what it feels
To lead a content life
When you don't know
if you exist
Or are waiting
to be born.

DIVE

Teal and turquoise
Spilling into each other
Beckon bewitchingly

Yielding
I dive right in
From a cliff above
A thousand feet
Free falling through the sky
My life flashes before my eye
Until I hit the water
And suddenly I am unborn
As the ocean engulfs me
Into its pristine womb
Drawing me to its depths
So full of life
It's vastness and silence
Pouring into me
With a deafening roar

Sunlight fades
I can't see anymore
The weight of the ocean
Presses me down
I go deeper
Into the water
And within myself
I am reborn
And released

From my personal hell
I gasp,
Suddenly I am awake
In that instant
In the place
Where I belong
Out in the deep sea
This is true home!

Alas, I rise to the surface
Pushed up
By unseen hands
Clearly some work to be done
Before I return
Floating now
Warm sun on my face
I've lived another life
I'll die another time
Of all the times
I have been born
How fortunate I am
To be an ocean spawn

.

The Date

She came looking for me
Knocking at my door
With those wise eyes
Boring into my soul.
All my actions - good and bad,
my words, half-truths, untold lies
Lay naked and threadbare
Sifted through a sieve of despair.
I was on a date with myself
Many decades too late
Getting to know me
Through someone else.
Someone from the past
From lifetimes before
Someone who loved me
Yet was keeping score.

No place to run, nowhere to hide
I accepted my fate and turned around.
Karma had arrived
Bounty Hunter from the past
She was waiting for me
To hand me my cross.
She is neither vengeful
Nor is she an angel
She won't set you free
Till you settle your debt
With her master
Also known as destiny.

The Willows

I walked past a beautiful house
nestled in the midst of weeping willows
Did the house grow the willows,
or did the willows plant the house, I wondered
A beautiful stately manor,
Wrapped within shaded arched verandas
Holding it in its embrace.
Rattan chairs stretched out by a large wooden table
With an exquisite vase
Holding an assortment of asters, ferns, peony, tiger lilies
And a perfect tea service waiting for its people.
The house had such a noble air and was so familiar
I wondered if I'd been here.
The mellow warmth of the afternoon sun
With a few beams breaking through the scattered clouds
Lit up the house from above
Casting an ethereal glow
The setting was perfect
But somehow it didn't belong there-
The windows and doors
All openly inviting drew me towards it
And I walked into a peaceful, orderly calmness.
It was quiet.
A lived-in house with no one around.
Neither abandoned nor occupied.
Like someone holding their breath in anticipation,
a still life, frozen midway.
I walked from room to room
Each beautifully appointed

Shelves filled with exquisite things
Precious almost.
My eyes fell upon a silver paper knife
Like the one I had gifted to someone,
a pair of earrings that I got in return,
a book here,
a scarf there,
a painting,
a trinket.

Everything I saw and touched
Had touched me before.
Room after room full of things,
And memories-
A walk by the shoreline,
A night spent watching the ebb of waves on a rock,
An early morning ride.
A memory of a dance without movement
Of a song without words.
A dinner that didn't need a conversation
And a conversation made up of glances.
Memories lined up like clothes on a hanger
Some laid out neatly like clothes for the evening,
Waiting for its people to come and wear them.

I wander from room to room,
walking through what felt
Like my memory palace of love
Searching for the ones who live here-
For the owners, claimants, creators
Of love's remembrance,
For the weavers of this net of emotions
That had collected these memories

Lying undisturbed.

I search every room
for what seemed an eternity
puzzled,
willing for someone to appear,
something to change.

And then,
an epiphany!

This was not a house I was walking through,
It was my heart-
And it was empty.

Saudade

How bitter yet sweet
It is to be reminded
Of a memory,
of a notion
That doesn't exist.

That fleeting feeling
That defies description-
No word can capture
Nor an emotion contain.
It waltzes into your mind
A constant refrain
And crushes you
In an obsessive embrace.
You hold your breath,
And will yourself
To reach out and grasp
At a silhouette.

But my love,
can't you see
You can't dance
forever
With an invisible
partner.

Days Without End

Days without end
Nights without beginning
I lie captured
Somewhere in between.

Silver sands
Bathed in moonlight
Midnight skies
Pierced by starlight.

I lie captured
In the hues of light
As it seeps through the horizon
Dissolving boundaries
Merging noon and night.

I lie captured
Deep within time
At the edge of eternity
Waiting to be set free.

R AIN

What does it feel like to be rain?
To fall gently onto the earth
Only to evaporate,
Vanish like a lover after a tryst
Leaving no trace of yourself
Unless you know where to look
Maybe on a leaf, glistening
With the last rays of the sun
Captured within like an illusion

Or immerse yourself in soil
And emerge
As a fragrance,
Intimate and haunting
To be inhaled deeply and
Etched forever into memory

What does it feel like
To collect yourself
In crevices and shallows
Lying patiently in wait
To create a new life
Or provide succour for
An existing one

Or what does it feel like
To fall violently and furiously
Broken free
From the captivity of clouds

Lashing out thunderously
On helpless vessels out at sea
Pounding them
Until the ocean pities their torment
And engulfs them
To forever lie on her soft sandy bed

Or to bear down on the ground
Splitting it and pushing it
Down the vast mountain face
Felling the majestic pines and cedars
Relentlessly, persistently

Or to fall on the marble archway
Only to shatter into a thousand drops
Exorcised of its power and malice
Spent of all its potent rage
Lying benign,
Looking up at the sky
Seeking its absent captor
Only to realize
She was at once
Both the cage and it's prisoner.

Memory

The tenderness of the new leaf is bewitching
The lightness of the green so different
From the hardened green of mature leaves
That have witnessed and weathered so much.
I look hard, and yet fail to find beauty in age
The luminosity, stupidity, spontaneity and frivolity of youth
Is decayed by wisdom and weariness of experience.
Is it possible to recapture the essence of what we once were, how we felt?
The realization of diminishing possibilities,
Of unrealized dreams and
Of unfulfilled potential
Crushes you.

And yet, a moment- nuanced and subtle-comes along
Like a gentle breeze
That parts the curtains briefly and allows us to feel something familiar,
Something you ought to know,
Which lies just beneath the consciousness.

You know it's there -
You grasp at it-
Clutching at wisps that your memory throws at you
You try,
But alas,
Who can contain mercury in a sieve,
Or capture the atoms of dust suspended in the rays of light?
The ray's purpose is to show you that the atoms exist.

The atom's purpose is to elude you,
Till you stop reaching out for it.

It will come to you-
Settle on you and within you,
In that moment
when you are still and aware.
When you start to rise up slowly
From the depths of your consciousness
Carefully untangling yourself
From all the constructs
that contain you
And you become the dust,
When you become the leaf
When you become love
And everything within.

Slowing Down

I stopped running one day after years
And just stood still.
Suddenly I became aware
Of where I was- on a long straight road
Stretching endlessly into oblivion.
A few people were running
Alone like me
Focused, and looking straight ahead
Determination and purpose
Writ large on their faces
They all looked the same
Yet none were familiar.
I was alone and by myself,
I was ahead of everyone I knew
I was even ahead
Of the ambitions I had set.
Appears that I had left behind
My friends, my passions
My hobbies
And even my family.
I couldn't run back-
That was not allowed
A tiny voice at the back of my head informed
So I just stood there and looked about.
It wasn't desolate, or depressing-far from it!
The bright sun was on my face
And around me a pleasant breeze.
I saw a small garden with a single tall shady tree
And a welcoming bench beneath.

I looked ahead and behind
And every few miles or so,
By the side of the road
Small gardens were laid out
With ponds and benches around
Something I had missed
in my race to nowhere.

I went into the garden
and sat on the bench
At times it's good to take stock
Of what you gained,
and where you lost.

So, I looked at the blades of grass
and the distant horizon
And waited
for all the things that mattered
to catch up
And go along with me
For the rest of the journey.

Full Circle

Dusk sets in slowly and gently,
Gathering to her bosom
All that Dawn had scattered
As she burst through the fading night.

Dawn, much like a young girl,
Skipping through the skies,
Endearingly self-absorbed,
Seemingly clumsy,
Jumps into puddles of clouds
And watches,
As they flit away lazily and
Arrange themselves again
into curious kaleidoscopic patterns.
Others dissipate
and settle as dew drops
On long blades of grass
Or descend as mist.
This is a routine they are used to
And watch nonchalantly
As she twirls around,
Lost in her own thoughts,
Gently sending a breeze towards the orchards,
Waking up the birds roosting within trees.
She skips away gaily into the west,
Oblivious of the lives she has awakened,
Dreams of the previous night
still weighing heavily in their eyes.

Morning arrives with steely efficiency,
Like a dashing young Captain-
intense, powerful, bright
Radiating promise, capability, intent and good looks,
Marching to the accompaniment of a grand orchestra.
It is difficult to not be enamoured by his heat and shimmer,
For being with him is to feel alive and adventurous.
With keen eyes absorbing everything in his realm,
He starts to spin life,
Slowly at first like a meditative dervish,
Gradually increasing to a crescendo of activity.
The world is his carousel
and he is the master spinner of stories and dreams-
Of dizzying spires and majestic cathedrals,
Of industry and scientific discoveries,
Of fortune and conquest,
Of glory and victory.
Enchanted beings clamour to get onto this ride-
To be part of this spinning vortex,
To be caught in this frenzy of creation,
Hearts thumping, eyes glazed,
Dizzy with desire,
Uncaring of the danger,
As they see beings flung out
And disappear into other worlds
soundlessly,
Their screams caught in their throat,
Shock and realization writ on their face.
Slowly the carousel spends itself
Into a bearable pace,
And the beings stagger out
Feeling invincible and drunk with power
They survived what lesser mortals couldn't.

Realization is still many births and spins away.
Morning is amused
And the more amused he gets
The more magnificent he becomes,
Scorching almost!
He will be back
With newer tests of endurance
To keep pushing them to the brink,
till they learn to get off the carousel
And not be flung off.
But will they?
The more evolved beings know better
Than to get entangled with morning,
and watch from the skies and from the soil.
The less evolved will take many births.
Morning is a charming hustler,
Engaging and addictive,
But routinely destructive.
He is the ultimate gambling den-
you can play all you want,
But in the end,
the house always wins.

Afternoon slinks in like a moody, sullen teenager
Unnoticed while the beings are still gathering their wits
And recovering from their tryst
with morning and all that he left in his wake.
Unnoticed, till a subtle shift is sensed in the air
As she makes her presence felt.
Suddenly the air feels heavy and oppressive,
The mind feels leaden,
A dark abyss opens up
As if to suck up the collective energy.

Afternoon is pensive as she tries to make sense of herself.
She is at once a childish adult
And a troubled rebellious teen
In search of her identity.
Right now, she feels like a placeholder,
A stop-gap,
Without purpose
Or reason.
She is not beautiful or carefree like dawn,
Eagerly awaited with her freshness and dew drops and promise.
She is not like morning - all swashbuckling charm.
So, what is she?
What is she going to be?
What does she mean?
The self-doubt rages within as she unleashes herself-
Sometimes with rain,
Sometimes scorching heat,
Sometimes thunder,
Sometimes emptiness.
Her rage explodes onto everything,
But it's a petty rage,
Still not fully formed,
Not lethal or powerful enough to be frightening,
Not yet grown up
It's an attention-seeking, stomping of feet, and banging of doors kind of fury.
Best endured patiently.
Best waited out.

Dusk! Beautiful imperial Dusk.
She glides in slowly and gently,
Like a stately ship sailing into port,
Gathering to her bosom

All that Dawn had scattered
As she burst through the fading night,
All that Morning left spent in his wake,
And all that Afternoon tried to unhinge
In her petulant rage.
She is the vast blue ocean of the skies-
Mystical and hypnotic-
Seeping towards the horizon.
She is the warmth of the yellow light
And the romance of a string quartet.
She watches as the weary return to their solace.
Above, in the sky a million stars appear
Their light reflected in the lamps on earth,
As if to show solidarity with the stars above,
Their glow indicating they are part of the same star.
Dusk is ready to welcome her Queen.

Night, the Queen rides in
Like a resplendent bride decked in black
Celestial moon dust, planets and stars
Willfully held captive in her unending train.
The sky is her bridal bed
and she commands it in dazzling splendour.
If Morning was about manipulation and conquest,
Night is about seduction and surrender.
She is the sensuousness of a bare shoulder,
The elegance of a long-stemmed rose,
She is the warmth of a fireplace
and desire in a lover's eyes.
She is the intimacy of a gaze held too long,
and of a dance too close,
The illicitness of forbidden love
and the yearning of an unrequited one.

She is the thrill of a whispered assignation,
and of yielding to the inevitable.
She is the passion of love
and the pleasure of loving.
She is the ravishing Queen under whose canopy a million kings have been vanquished.

When all has been said and done
The Queen looks east for her reprieve
At Dawn,
who comes skipping through the skies.

SPACE

Deep, dark and serene
Eternal womb,
Birther of destiny
Billions of offspring contained within
Where do you end,
When did you begin?

Question

Generations of stars
So many heavenly beings
Born from each other
Or out of nothing
Silently revolving
Their orbits ordained
Undisturbed
By meteors and comets
That come tearing through space
Like playful children
Chasing each other
Through this vast playground
Noiseless flashes
Before disappearing altogether

Somewhere in the deep
A star dies
Elsewhere
Another is born
And a constellation is formed
This celestial metropolis
Collapsing and expanding
Forever changing
Yet beautifully static

And in a far corner
On a tiny speck
An ant asks its mother
As it looks at skyscrapers

The same thought
That plagues humans
As they look at the sky
And seeks answers
For questions
They struggle to frame

Instead, they ask
How vast is endless
And how long is eternity
Where do they belong
Who else is out there
What is their place
And how does this end

Who answers the ants' question?
Who answers yours?
What will you do
About your existential angst?

Still

I'm so far from where
I need to be
But how can I get there
If I'm forever moving?

I wander
from place to place
Searching for answers
To questions unformed
Tripping over thoughts
And for the curtain to part

Perhaps
The most extraordinary journey
Starts by being still
and in one place,
And the greatest distance
Is covered
When you travel
to the heart from mind
Conquering
both space and time.

Moon

The sun receded
Growing shadows long,
The night sky
Crept softly in,
Like a caress,
And feathers on skin.

A gentle breeze
Swept through leaves,
a whisper of tenderness
And long forgotten memories.

The moon lay on the horizon,
Sensuous and languid,
Waiting for her lover
To rouse her
And travel through the stars.

Down below
A million people sighed
The moon reflected
In their own desire.

The Key

Music wafts in,
Key to a forgotten memory,
Of a world lived
In a different life.

Two people,
look up startled
As images escape
The unlocked box
Rising slowly
To waltz with the notes
Whispering secrets
That they each know.

Two people
Lost, and now found
Reach out
Beyond time and space
Across parallel realms
Soulmates –
Now, Before,
And Forever.

Thoughts

I was emptiness
Watching myself

Till my watching
Became a thing

A thing
That turned to thought
And the thought
Watched itself
Till it became a thing
That turned to thought

And on
And on
It went
Till my emptiness
Became full
Littered with things
That became thoughts

Wherever I glanced
I fell into a thought

A thought so deep
It took me
A thousand years
To emerge from it

Each time I rose
I fell
Again
And again
Till I closed my eyes
And stopped
watching

Slowly the emptiness
Returned
And filled the cavern
Of thoughts
And one by one
Closed them out

Now it's just me
Alone
At peace
In my Vast Empty.

You Write. We Publish.

To publish your own book, contact us.

We publish poetry collections, short story collections, novellas and novels.

contact@thewriteorder.com

Instagram- thewriteorder

www.facebook.com/thewriteorder

www.ingramcontent.com/pod-product-compliance
Lightning Source LLC
LaVergne TN
LVHW041621070526
838199LV00052B/3206